MELBOURNE
VICTORIA

Above: The Yarra River, Flinders Street Station and Melbourne's glittering towers.
Left: Lights dazzle from the spired Victorian Arts Centre. To its left is the National Gallery of Victoria. In the foreground is the Yarra River.

SPARKLING MELBOURNE

A city for night-time celebration

Melbourne published its first newspaper weather map in 1881, and the city's inhabitants have been very aware of their city's pleasant climate, with its temperate summers and cool, energising winters, ever since. Outdoor pleasures are at a premium in Melbourne, especially in the warmer months. At night, the city glitters and gleams with light and is alive with people dining out, taking in a show, or simply enjoying a promenade and seeing the sights. There is plenty to do in city and inner suburbs at night and theatres, restaurants, cafes and nightclubs offer fare and entertainment to suit all tastes.

Stylish Collins Street glows at dusk.

Marvellous Melbourne

"O Sweet Queen-city of the Golden South,
Piercing the evening with thy starlit spires...
I saw the parallels of thy long streets
With lamps like angels shining all a-row..."

Patrick Moloney, writing of Melbourne, 1879

Top: Flinders Street Station against a fiery twilight.
Above: The illuminated spire of the Victorian Arts Centre.
Right: "Australia's most liveable city" in jewelled glory.

4

FLINDERS STREET STATION

"We'll meet under the clocks…"

Flinders Street Station, built on the site of an earlier terminus, was completed in 1910, and its appearance pays tribute to the gracious architecture of the later Victorian era. The station is a hub for Victoria's excellent railway network and the clocks over the main entrance, a traditional Melbourne meeting-place, show departure times for trains on a variety of lines. The station presides over the crossroads of the city, where Swanston Street, the main north-south thoroughfare, intersects Flinders Street, which runs along the bank of the Yarra River and is the southern boundary of Melbourne's central business district.

VICTORIAN ARTS CENTRE

Melbourne's great cultural complex

A short walking distance over Princes Bridge from Melbourne city centre, in St Kilda Road, is Melbourne's magnificent arts complex. First stage to be built was the National Gallery of Victoria, opened in 1968 and noted for its collection of Old Masters, as well as for contemporary works of art. The Victorian Arts Centre, which stands next to the gallery, was opened in 1984. Crowned by a spectacular spire, this performing arts venue includes the State Theatre (home to the Australian Ballet and to the Australian Opera Company), the Playhouse and the George Fairfax Studio. On the river side of the theatres, and next to Westgate, is the superb Melbourne Concert Hall, which seats 2,600 people.

Far left: Fairy-lights frame the Victorian Arts Centre spire.
Left above, left and below: Three aspects of the spectacular spire of the Victorian Arts Centre.

Above: Southgate (left) on the Yarra offers dining and promenading.
Left: The Princess Theatre in Spring Street, now brilliantly renovated,
was established in 1854 at the height of the Victorian gold-rush.
Inset far left: Eating outdoors is a pleasure in Melbourne.
Inset left: An elegant Melbourne restaurant awaits diners.

OUT AND ABOUT

A city in which to have fun

Melbourne city, and its adjoining suburban "villages", such as St Kilda, Fitzroy and Carlton, offer a stunning choice of venues for shopping and entertainments. There are over 2,000 restaurants in the area, offering a wide variety of national cuisines. Carlton's Lygon Street is especially famous for its Italian food, and Little Bourke Street is the place for Asian fare. Melbourne people love celebrations and happily gather in the city's spacious parklands and other public places for holidays, festivals, or just to have fun together.

Carols by candlelight, in the Sidney Myer Music Bowl in Kings Domain.

The peaceful St Kilda Pier will become a crowded thoroughfare on the weekend.

Eating out in Melbourne can be as informal as the diner chooses.

DINING AND SHOPPING IN STYLE
Ways to enjoy Melbourne

Whatever the heart desires can be found in Melbourne, that great multicultural metropolis where fine wares from all over the world are displayed in a diversity of marketplaces. What better way to spend time in Melbourne than shopping and sightseeing in Collins Street, or in Southgate's boutiques, or in Bourke Street Mall, or Royal Arcade, or in the marvellous Melbourne Central complex, "the life of the city"? After shopping, dine at one of Melbourne's great restaurants. The weekend can bring a trip to St Kilda, to stroll its pier and to visit cafes and markets.

Above: Melbourne is noted for outstanding Italian cuisine.
Opposite: main picture: Melbourne Central has 180 specialty shops and an international department store.
Opposite: inset above and below: Nineteenth-century Royal Arcade; historic Shot Tower inside Melbourne Central.

Como House, part of which dates to 1847, is a colonial mansion set in fine gardens..

Parliament House, in Spring Street, was built in 1856.

MELBOURN

A modern city with a sense of history

Established and consolidated within the reign of Queen Victoria (1837-1901), Melbourne has been described as "one of the finest examples of a Victorian city remaining anywhere in the world". Many of its cathedrals, theatres, hotels, public buildings and mansions were financed by wealth from gold, from primary production such as wool, and from commerce. Today, the National Trust of Australia (Victoria) is actively concerned with properties such as Como House at South Yarra, a fine example of the town residences built by the "squattocracy" in the second half of the nineteenth century, Latrobe's Cottage in Kings Domain (home of the State's first Lieutenant-Governor from 1839 to 1854), Rippon Lea at Elsternwick (construction begun in 1868) and Old Melbourne Gaol (1851).

Right: traditional and modern Melbourne: St Michael's Church and the Hyatt Hotel.

Melbourne's Public Baths stand on the corner of Victoria and Swanston Streets.

Smart terrace houses are a feature of Melbourne's inner suburbs.

The Armorial Bearings of the Corporation of Melbourne date to 1843.
The motto means "We gather strength as we go".

The Grand Postal Hall of Melbourne's General Post Office.

OLD & NEW

Opposite: main picture: Flowers and a decorated tram brighten St Kilda Road.
Inset left: Artworks add colour to Melbourne city streets.
Inset right: Even city light poles become works of art in Melbourne.

Above: Light Horsemen ride past one of Melbourne's famous trams towards the Shrine of Remembrance.
Left: A carriage and pair provides a gracious and traditional way to see Melbourne city.

A CITY WITH A STYLE ALL ITS OWN

Many of Melbourne's grand buildings were constructed as a result of the nineteenth-century gold-rushes and subsequent rural prosperity. Today, ornamented and opulent, they stand side-by-side with more modern, sleeker towers, in streets lined by European trees, whose leaves take on autumn-bronze, fall in colourful profusion, then are renewed in springtime green. Even narrow-fronted terrace houses have their gardens, their greenery, and blossoms which echo the grand floral displays of the magnificent public parks.

Melbourne's wide boulevards and orderly traffic allow reminders of earlier, more leisurely eras, such as horse-drawn carriages, to take part in the city's busy life. Sharing the roads are Melbourne's famous trams, whose decorated panels often bear witness to the city's passion for art, which finds expression in a multitude of galleries and in more public displays on pavements and other open-air venues.

In the Conservatory, Fitzroy Gardens.   *A dazzling display of flowers in Kings Domain.*   *Marquis of Linlithgow statue, Kings Domain.*

GREEN SPACES AND FLORAL BEAUTY

Melbourne's early settlers established the tradition of beautifying the city's streets with trees and reserved large areas of land for public parks and gardens. Verdant Fitzroy Gardens features a Conservatory, the sculptured Fairy Tree and a model Tudor Village, as well as Captain Cook's Cottage, transported to Melbourne in 1934 from Great Ayton, in North Yorkshire, England.

The beautiful Royal Botanic Gardens, near the city heart and over 35.4 hectares in extent, was created in the English landscaping tradition of the eighteenth century, and contains the National Herbarium. Kings Domain contains Government House and the Shrine of Remembrance, Latrobe's Cottage (built in 1839) and the Sidney Myer Music Bowl. Carlton Gardens surrounds the Royal Exhibition Buildings and the largest of Melbourne's open parklands, Royal Park, covers 180 hectares and offers sporting facilities.

Above: main picture: The Yarra flows past (left) Royal Botanic Gardens and Government House and (right) Olympic Park and the National Tennis Centre.
Opposite: St Patrick's Roman Catholic Cathedral (foreground) was built in Gothic style in 1858. Also shown (above) are the Houses of Parliament and then Bourke Street.
Opposite: inset left to right: The Royal Exhibition Building; Melbourne's parks are noted for splendid floral displays; relaxing in Melbourne's Royal Botanic Gardens.

Captain Cook's Cottage stands in Fitzroy Gardens.

"... by very skilful disposition of lawns, the layout of paths, the use of water and above all the placing of specimen trees, the Royal Botanic Gardens, Melbourne, presents itself as a long series of landscape pictures - vistas, panoramas, prospects and perspectives of quite exceptional beauty."

Edward Hyams: "Great Botanic Gardens of the World"

Above: Melbourne's gardens are places for quiet relaxation.
Opposite: The Conservatory in Fitzroy Gardens.

The Shrine of Remembrance and Perpetual Flame at dusk.

THE SHRINE OF REMEMBRANCE

"At the going-down of the sun ..."

Melbourne's stately Shrine of Remembrance was built as a tribute to the men and women who served in World War One. It was designed so that on Armistice Day, at the eleventh hour of the eleventh day of the eleventh month each year, a ray of sunlight strikes the Rock of Remembrance in the inner sanctuary. The Forecourt of the Shrine was built in 1952, in memory of the fallen from World War Two. The Shrine now commemorates all who have served their country in times of war.

Left: A view over the Shrine of Remembrance, looking down St Kilda Road to Swanston Street and central Melbourne city.

Top: Princes Bridge, moored ferries and a lone sculler grace the Yarra River.
Above: A lovely summer twilight beside the sparkling Yarra.

BESIDE THE YARRA
Melbourne's own river

In 1837, an overland traveller wrote of Melbourne that "The site of the town is very pretty and well chosen... on the Yarra Yarra River...". Since then, the Yarra has continued to be the heart of Melbourne, its meandering course "straightened" in 1897, and its green banks alternately built-upon and beautified over the years. Today, the river flows quietly through the city, past the impressive Southgate complex, its shining surface mirroring reflections of bridges, barbecues and bicycle-paths, its placidity broken by business-like ferries and shells sculled by energetic rowers.

Right: Southgate complex extends along the Yarra west from Princes Bridge.
Right near inset: A bright sculpture at Southgate, beside the Yarra.
Right far inset: Giant fish circle in a stairwell at Southgate.
Following pages: The Yarra River reflects Melbourne's shining skyline.

BRIDGES TO ADVENTURE
Journeys in space & in the heart

Melbourne is a city from which to set out on grand expeditions, and also on smaller, more personal journeys of discovery. The three bridges across the Yarra pictured here are gateways to varied adventures.

Below: Westgate Bridge spans the Yarra on the highway from Melbourne to Geelong and points west. It is 2.6 kilometres long and has a navigational clearance of 52 metres.

Footbridge from Southgate to Flinders Walk.

Westgate Bridge, major link with Princes Freeway and Highway One, resounds to approximately 100,000 vehicles travelling west from Melbourne or returning to the city each day. Princes Bridge receives St Kilda Road traffic and channels it to Swanston and Flinders Streets, linking the city directly to its southern suburbs. The charming footbridge linking Southgate with Flinders Walk is a favourite venue for wedding photographers, who capture the beginnings of another of life's journeys!

Princes Bridge (right), Flinders Street Station (centre) and the Melbourne skyline.

The Queen Victoria Market was officially opened in 1879.

Decoration over entrance to Queen Victoria Market.

"Polly Woodside" Maritime Park is on the Yarra in South Melbourne.

The "Polly Woodside" is a beautifully-restored three-masted barque.

Cell block at Old Melbourne Gaol, scene of 104 hangings and now a penal museum.

Ned Kelly was executed at Old Melbourne Gaol in 1880.

PAST MEMORIES, PRESENT DELIGHTS
Of "Polly", Ned, Queen Victoria and others

Melbourne is full of memories of the past and historic institutions which have been adapted to the demands of today. The "Polly Woodside" Maritime Park offers memories of the days when Melbourne was home to tall ships and showcases a splendid vessel, built in 1885 and beautifully restored. Old Melbourne Gaol, which dates to 1841 and was closed in 1923, brings shivers to the spine with mementoes of Ned Kelly and others who paid the law's penalties within its grim walls. For entertainment and a choice of wonderful local produce and other wares, the Queen Victoria Market, with its bantering stallholders, is the place to visit.

Asian Small-clawed Otters provide endless entertainment for visitors to Melbourne Zoo.

Melbourne Zoo is home to magnificent Sumatran Tigers.

The zoo has had success in breeding the Lowland Gorilla.

The Japanese Garden is very popular with visitors.

This Syrian Bear is part of a popular breeding group.

THE ROYAL MELBOURNE ZOOLOGICAL GARDENS
A home to creatures great and small

Melbourne Zoo was opened in 1862 and today is a popular city attraction. The grounds are splendidly landscaped and areas are planted so that groups of animals can be seen in surroundings closely resembling their natural habitats. The zoo is home to more than 350 different sorts of Australian and exotic animals and has had notable success in breeding some of the world's endangered species, such as the Lowland Gorilla. Highlights of a visit to the zoo will include the Butterfly House, the Gorilla Rainforest, the Sumatran Tiger Rainforest and the Treetops Exhibit, as well as viewing Australia's unique Platypus and Koala.

The Melbourne Cricket Ground is the venue for the annual Australian Football Grand Final.

A SPORTING CITY
Melburnians love a hard-fought game

Perhaps the sporting instincts of the people of Melbourne trace to the goldfields era and its influx of men and women willing to stake all on fortune's whim. Certainly the Olympic Games of 1956 gave fresh impetus to a fascination with sport which had already found expression in Victoria's very own game, a football code which has become known as Australian Football.

Opposite: An aerial clash in an Australian Football match.

"They're off!" in the Melbourne Cup at Flemington Racecourse.

Victoria's Paul Reiffel bowling in a cricket match at the Melbourne Cricket Ground.

Whatever the reason, Melbourne today can lay fair claim to being Australia's most sports-oriented city, with today's Australian Football Grand Final packing around 100,000 exhilarated fans into the Melbourne Cricket Ground. The M.C.G. was the main stadium for the 1956 Olympics. Today, it is the venue for top-grade State and international cricket in summer. Nearby, at Flinders Park is the splendid National Tennis Centre, while Olympic Park is a venue for soccer, rugby and athletics. The Melbourne Cup is a nation-stopping event which climaxes the Spring Racing Carnival on the first Tuesday of each November.

"Puffing Billy" travels 13 kilometres from Belgrave to Emerald Lake.

"Puffing Billy" is the State's oldest original steam locomotive.

THE DANDENONG RANGES
A green haven

Thirty-two kilometres from Melbourne, the Dandenong Ranges offer a diversity of refuges from the busy city life. Dandenong Ranges National Park was declared in 1987 and amalgamated Fern Tree Gully Forest (a reserve since 1882), Sherbrooke and Doongalla Forests. Mount Dandenong, the range's highest point at 633 metres, is an old volcanic peak. Deep fern gullies and forests of tall trees, including the towering mountain ash, offer space to relax and observe wildlife including the Superb Lyrebird. The ranges are famous for their gardens, plant nurseries, art galleries and antique stores. To experience the area's charm in full, take a journey from Belgrave to Emerald Lake on "Puffing Billy", whose carriages are pulled by Victoria's oldest steam locomotive.

A pair of Red Kangaroos at Healesville Sanctuary.

Feeding a pair of Australian Pelicans at Healesville Sanctuary.

A Dingo meets a young admirer at Healesville Sanctuary.

Healesville Sanctuary is noted for its flourishing Koala colony.

HEALESVILLE SANCTUARY
Caring for Australia's wildlife

For over fifty years, Healesville Sanctuary has been committed to the care of Australian wildlife. Over the years, the Sanctuary has bred many species of Australian animals and today is involved in breeding programmes for more than 20 species classified as threatened. Care is provided for orphaned or injured animals, many of which are returned to the wild. Healesville is 65 kilometres from Melbourne and provides a truly Australian experience, where the visitor can stroll through groups of kangaroos and wallabies and view many other unique Australian species of animals, including Koalas, Platypuses and magnificent birds of prey, at close quarters.

Trams take merrymakers right to St Kilda's Luna Park.

AROUND PORT PHILLIP BAY
Having fun along the waterfront

Almost under the shadow of Westgate Bridge in Spotswood, where the Yarra River flows into Port Phillip Bay, is the fascinating Science Works, the science and technology centre of the Museum of Victoria. South of Spotswood is Williamstown, whose northern aspect is a feast for the maritime-minded, including sailing clubs, marinas, piers and H.M.S. *Castlemaine*, Maritime Museum Ship. Across the Yarra entrance, along the northern shores of the bay, is famed St Kilda, where fun-seekers can promenade the pier, cycle or rollerblade, visit Luna Park, or dine formally or alfresco at some of Melbourne's best eating-places.

Melbourne's skyline seen through masts from St Kilda Pier.

Above: St Kilda Pier. Opposite: main picture: An aerial view of Williamstown. Inset left and right: Science Works, the Victorian Museum's Science and Technology Centre.

FUN BY THE BAY

Escaping from it all

Port Phillip Bay is Melbourne's playground. The blue water and fine beaches offer a multitude of ways in which Melburnians and visitors can relax and enjoy themselves. The northern shoreline is decorated with seaside suburbs, while further southwards towns are spaced along the scenic coast and look inland to a hinterland of peaceful and productive rural activities. Swimming, surfing, sailing, snorkeling and scuba-diving, fishing, powerboating, beachcombing, birdwatching, sealwatching - the recreational possibilities of the Bay are seemingly endless. Bayside towns such as Sorrento, Rosebud, and Queenscliff have been holiday destinations since Victorian times and today offer entertainments and accommodation suitable for daytrippers and longterm vacationers. Sometimes, however, it is the simpler occupations which are most satisfying, such as sitting quietly in the winter sunshine outside one of the famous bathing boxes on Brighton Beach.

Right and below: Bathing-boxes at Brighton, on Port Phillip Bay.

PHILLIP ISLAND

Seascapes and sea-creatures on display

Phillip Island, 120 kilometres from Melbourne, lies across the entrance to Westernport Bay and has been a popular resort since the 1870s. It is accessible by bridge, after a scenic drive down the Bass Highway, although some prefer the ferry trip from Stony Point to Cowes. The island offers spectacular scenery and a wealth of wildlife. Favourites with visitors are the Little Penguins, which, during the breeding season that begins in August, brood their eggs in burrows in the sand-dunes. For about eight weeks after each chick hatches, one of its parents comes ashore each sunset to feed it, in a "parade" eagerly watched by visitors to the island. Australian Fur Seals also provide fascinating viewing for visitors to the island.

Left: A Phillip Island seascape.
Inset far left: Little Penguins coming to land at night to feed their chicks.
Inset left: A colony of Australian Fur Seals can be viewed from The Nobbies.
Below: The Little Penguin is the smallest of the world's penguins.

Point Nepean, at the end of the Mornington Peninsula.

The pier at Frankston, on the Mornington Peninsula.

Boardwalks allow safe viewing of Cape Schanck.

THE MORNINGTON PENINSULA
Playground for a city

The Mornington Peninsula is Melbourne's holiday mecca, with a seacoast studded with opulent holiday homes and busy resort towns, and a fertile hinterland. The Nepean Highway offers a direct route to the peninsula, but a more scenic drive begins at Port Melbourne and skirts seaside suburbs such as St Kilda on the way to Frankston. Then the coast road runs past Mornington, Dromana and Rosebud (take the chairlift to the top of Arthurs Seat for a great view), then on to Sorrento, Portsea and Point Nepean National Park, which was opened in 1988. A leisurely return will allow exploration of boutique wineries, art and craft centres and many wonderful restaurants.

Sorrento Pier, where the sun shines on Nature's beauty.

A view from Arthurs Seat.

Sorrento Back Beach.

Arthurs Seat Chair Lift.

Blairgowrie, on the narrow upturned "toe" of the Mornington Peninsula, is a wonderful place for holidaying.

Tapestry in Geelong's Wool Museum.

Shearing shed tableau in Geelong's Wool Museum.

The Wool Museum hosts Western District wool auctions.

GEELONG
Gateway to the Ballarine Peninsula

Only 72 kilometres from Melbourne, Geelong is Victoria's second-largest city. It contains many historic buildings (including the original Customs House, erected in 1838) and is noted for its lovely civic gardens. The first farmers brought sheep to Geelong in 1836 and the city's magnificent National Wool Museum celebrates "the fleece that built Australia". Set on Corio Bay, Geelong is Victoria's leading port after Melbourne and its history is displayed in the Port of Geelong Authority's Maritime Museum.

Top: The National Wool Museum in Geelong is housed in a bluestone wool store built in 1872.
Below left and right: Geelong's Corio Bay, a sheltered haven; parks extend along Geelong's waterfront.

Queenscliff has been a seaside resort for over 100 years.

Fishing from Queenscliff Pier is a serious business.

Point Lonsdale Lighthouse is a vital navigational aid.

FROM QUEENSCLIFF TO POINT LONSDALE
Looking seawards

The southern coast of the Bellarine Peninsula offers historic and recreational interest. In 1860, because of fears of a Russian invasion, cannon were placed on the cliff top at Queenscliff, on Shortlands Bluff, overlooking "The Rip" which swirls between Port Phillip Heads. In 1863, the "Black" and "White" Lighthouses were constructed, and in the early 1880s Fort Queenscliff was erected. Queenscliff today contains beautifully-restored historic buildings. Its neighbour, Point Lonsdale, guards "The Rip" with a lighthouse standing 120 metres above sea-level, whose light is visible for 30 kilometres out to sea.

Below: Fort Queenscliff's Black Lighthouse was built of bluestone in 1863.
Right: Gun emplacement at Fort Queenscliff dates from the Crimean War.

GREAT OCEAN ROAD

A great achievement

In early 1916, Mr W. Calder proposed to the State War Council that a road should be built from Barwon Heads to Warrnambool by soldiers returned from World War One. Work on the road began in 1918 and it was opened on 26 November 1932, a tribute to the skills of engineer Major W. T. B. McCormack and a magnificent achievement by men working without modern mechanical assistance to tame the rocky, crumbling and often steeply sloping limestone hillsides of "the indented coast". Today, sealed and meticulously maintained, the Great Ocean Road is a pathway to the magic of some of Australia's most spectacular coastline and loveliest forested ranges.

Right: main picture: Fairhaven Beach lies on a coast noted for surf.
Right: insets top left and clockwise: Watch out for wildlife on the Great Ocean Road; Cape Otway Lighthouse was constructed after the tragic wreck of the "Cataraqui" in 1845; Split Point Lighthouse is locally known as "the White Lady"; Apollo Bay is a resort which is home to a large commercial fishing fleet.

"The Surf Coast" offers gentle seaside moments for family enjoyment, as well as world-class waves.

 THE OTWAY RANGES

Rainforest splendour

The Otway Ranges stretch from the town of Anglesea to Cape Otway, dropping to Bass Strait in the south and extending to the volcanic plains of the Colac region in the north. Averaging 2000 millimetres of rain in their southern section, they support forests of messmate, manna gum, blue gum and mountain grey gum and, at higher altitudes, the towering mountain ash and ancient myrtle beech. The ranges were logged heavily by timbergetters from 1848. Melba Gully State Park, noted today for its giant myrtle beech, was proclaimed in 1975 and is just west of Lavers Hill. Otway National Park, proclaimed in 1981, extends over most of the Cape Otway Peninsula and along the coastline to the west; Angahook-Lorne State Park, from Aireys Inlet to Kennett River, was declared in 1987. Picnic reserves and walks allow easy enjoyment of the wildlife and verdant beauty of these forest areas.

Left: main picture: Beautiful Erskine Falls are in Angahook-Lorne State Park. Left inset top to bottom: Crimson Rosella, common in the Otway Ranges; a bridge spans a clear rainforest creek in the Otway Ranges; Eastern Grey Kangaroo and joey may be seen in the Otways.

Hopetoun Falls, an exquisite cascade in the Otway Ranges.

The Tumble Coast

Kirrae,
Katubanut, Kolakgnat,
you knew the stories of the tumble coast,
where the sea eats up the land,
leaving
spirits watching,
alone with the wind.

Jaadwa,
Jarra and even Bungandiutj,
they've heard the stories too,
'bout the tumble coast
where islands disappear
and lonely spirits sail,
quietly
in the night,
when only the moon is watching.

Steve Parish

Main picture: Two of the famous Twelve Apostles.
Inset above: An aerial view of "the indented coast".
Inset above right: "London Bridge" before a 1990 collapse left the seaward arch isolated.

THE INDENTED COAST
Port Campbell National Park

From Princetown to Peterborough, the Great Ocean Road passes through Port Campbell National Park, renowned for its rugged and spectacular coastal landscape. Limestone cliffs drop sheer to the Southern Ocean, constantly sculpted by waves into stacks such as the famous Twelve Apostles. London Bridge, Razorback Rock, Mutton Bird Island, the Bakers Oven and the Grotto are only a few of the fascinating formations along this 32-kilometre stretch of coast. They, and the sites of some tragic shipwrecks, are accessible by roads and paths.

FROM WARRNAMBOOL TO PORT FAIRY
A maritime coast

Warrnambool, on Lady Bay, is Victoria's fifth-largest provincial city and the centre of a rich agricultural area. In the 1830s, whalers and sealers frequented the coast of Victoria. Today, Flagstaff Hill Maritime Village recreates these early seafaring days, and displays historic vessels and shipwreck relics, while Hopkins River Boat House offers more glimpses into nautical tradition. Port Fairy, 28 kilometres west of Warrnambool, originated as a whaling base and now has over 50 buildings classified by the National Trust.

Above: main picture: Boat Harbour, Port Fairy.
Inset, above left and clockwise: Hopkins River Boat House at Warrnambool; Flagstaff Hill Maritime Village is built around a lighthouse and 1887 fortifications at Warrnambool.

Shearing shed on a Murray River property.

RURAL VICTORIA
The wealth of the land

The west coast region of Victoria, from Geelong to the South Australian border, is noted for the production of fine wool, dairying and beef cattle and vegetable crops. Central Victoria, which once produced prodigious amounts of gold, is today known for wool, cattle and wine production. The Wimmera, in central western Victoria, produces grain and wool, while the northwest of the State, nearer to the Murray River, is known for wheat, wine and irrigated crops. To the mountainous northeast, the high country is surrounded by excellent farming land, used for sheep and cattle production. Beef cattle and merino sheep flourish in Gippsland, east of Melbourne, while dairying is a feature of East Gippsland. Mineral and timber production have accounted for much of Victoria's past wealth, but today rural industry, accompanied by a rapidly growing popular interest in farm holidays, continues to underwrite the State's prosperity.

Main picture: The wealth of the State of Victoria has long been in its agricultural and pastoral lands.
Inset left to right: Mustering sheep in the Western District; Herefords on a hillside near the High Country; moving a flock along a rural Victorian road.

Historic Montrose Cottage and Eureka Museum in Ballarat was built in 1856.

Cobb & Co coach at Sovereign Hill, Ballarat.

Houses in Ballarat retain a proud aura of colonial times.

Eureka Stockade is part of Australia's history.

GOLDEN TOWNS
Ballarat and Bendigo

On 20 August 1851, alluvial gold was discovered by Thomas Hiscock near Ballarat. Soon after, further discoveries were made near Bendigo. Would-be miners rushed to Victoria, and digging for gold and bushranging both became growth industries. By November 1854, the miners' grievances over enforcement of charges for mining licences reached flashpoint at Ballarat, with the storming of the Eureka Stockade by troopers and police. Today, Ballarat (population 78,300) is an imposing city, rich in fabulous Victorian buildings and magnificent gardens, where goldfields life has been recreated at Sovereign Hill and at Montrose Cottage. Another goldrush centre, Bendigo (population 66,000), also contains superb examples of Victorian architecture.

Above: main picture: The city of Ballarat today displays many historic buildings.
Opposite: A gorgeous fountain in Bendigo expresses the opulence of a gold-rush city.

The upper Murray River begins its journey across Australia's southeast.

THE RIVER MURRAY

Victoria's northern boundary

According to an Aboriginal legend, a man who chased a giant cod down the Murray sang the river into existence. The great waterway long provided sustenance for Aboriginal people: today it indirectly or directly influences the lives of a large number of Australians. It rises in the mountains between Canberra and the Victoria-New South Wales border, then flows more than 2,500 kilometres before it enters the Southern Ocean. For much of its length, its southern waterline forms the boundary between New South Wales and Victoria. For much of the nineteenth century, the river was a busy commercial waterway. By 1873, there were 240 vessels trading along the Murray and Echuca was a roaring port. Eventually, however, railways took over the trade and only in the late 1900s have the paddlewheelers returned to prominence, this time carrying tourists enjoying the splendours of Australia's mightiest river.

Left: main picture: Sunrise on Australia's mightiest river, the Murray.
Inset left to right: The area around Swan Hill, on the Murray River, is the largest stone-fruit-producing region in Victoria; river red gums grow on much of the Murray River floodplain; water-skiing on Lake Hume, one of four dams along the Murray; paddlewheelers at Echuca's red-gum wharf are popular attractions.

Above: Mount Bogong is Victoria's highest peak. Opposite: Snow gums grow above the snowline in Victoria's alps.

THE VICTORIAN ALPS
In the High Country

Alpine National Park is Victoria's largest and most spectacular national park, which includes the "Man from Snowy River" High Country, the Bogong High Plains and Mount Bogong. To its west is Mount Buffalo National Park. In winter, these and other spectacular areas in the Victorian Alps attract skiers to slopes which cater for downhill racing, cross-country skiing, tobogganing or just enjoyment on skis in a wonderful environment. Mount Buffalo, Mount Hotham, Falls Creek, Mount Buller and other alpine localities offer resorts and amenities for all sorts of winter sports. In springtime and summer, visitors can bushwalk, fish the lakes and streams, horseride, or relax and enjoy the wildlife, the stunning views and the mountain wildflowers.

At Victoria's alpine resorts, skiers of all grades can have fun.

Victoria's Alps offer a variety of winter sport experiences.

The Hattah Lakes, in Victoria's northwest, fill when the Murray River floods.

SPOTLIGHTING NATURAL BEAUTY
Victoria's National and State Parks

Many of Victoria's outstanding natural attractions are protected in National Parks, State and Coastal Parks. All provide facilities for visitors. Official Wilderness Areas include the Big Desert in the northwest of the State. Historic Sites preserve evidence of Victoria's history, State Forests cater for recreation as well as provide timber and Wildlife Sanctuaries allow viewing of wildlife at close quarters. In addition, Victoria offers Marine Parks and Reserves, Wildlife Reserves and many other special places to visit.

Opposite: Climbing Mount Arapiles.
Opposite: inset top left: Mount Arapiles State Park, west of Horsham, was once a bushranger hideout.
Opposite: inset bottom right: A spectacular formation in the Grampians' Wonderland Range.

Wilsons Promontory National Park is 225 kilometres southeast from Melbourne.

· A History of ·
MELBOURNE
VICTORIA

The area which was later to be the site of the city of Melbourne was home to the Aboriginal people for many thousands of years.

The English navigator Matthew Flinders entered Port Phillip on 23 April, 1800 and reported country suited to agriculture and sheep. On October 1803, two ships under the command of Captain David Collins arrived in Port Phillip, but no permanent settlement was made. In 1823, Hume and Hovell travelled overland to Corio Bay (identifying it as Western Port) and reported "one of the finest ... tracts of country yet known in Australia".

Residents of Van Dieman's Land realised the potential of the area and eventually, in 1834, Edward Henty "squatted" at Portland Bay. In 1835, John Batman sailed from Launceston to Port Phillip Bay and discovered "the place for a village" a little distance up the Yarra River.

Officialdom declared that Batman and those who arrived soon after him were trespassers, but finally, on 9 September 1836, Sir Richard Bourke, Governor of New South Wales, officially recognised the year-old settlement. In 1837, Governor Bourke visited Port Phillip and approved Robert Hoddle's plan for a town to be named Melbourne.

Wool and other rural products were shipped in quantity from the settlement on the Yarra. By 1841, the Melbourne area had nearly 4500 residents and by 1851 almost 23,000. On 5 August 1850, Victoria was formally declared a colony in its own right, separate from New South Wales.

In 1851, gold was discovered at Ballarat and at Bendigo. Victoria became the focus of gold-seekers from all over the world. Wealth poured into Melbourne and by 1861 there were just over 200,000 Europeans on the Victorian goldfields and the population of Victoria was around 540,000.

The remainder of the nineteenth century saw colony and city flourish. By Federation, in 1901, rivalry between Melbourne and Sydney was well-established and has continued ever since. During the twentieth century, Melbourne has continued to develop and today, as it faces the twenty-first century, it is one of the world's great cities, a centre of culture, commerce and industry, with a quintessential Australian character that is the richer because of the multiculturalism that has gone into its making.